Odd Boy Out

YOUNG ALBERT EINSTEIN

by Don Brown

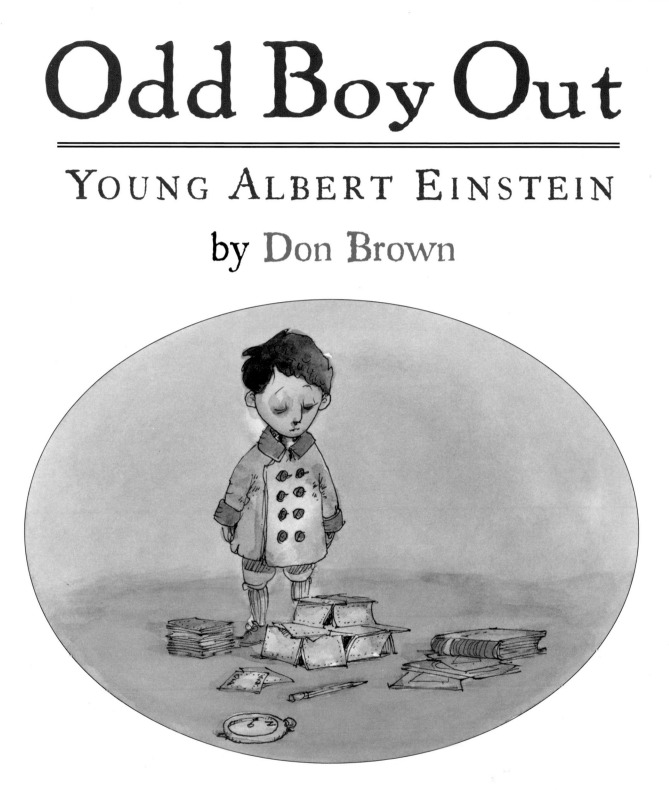

HOUGHTON MIFFLIN COMPANY • BOSTON

www.houghtonmifflinbooks.com

The text of this book is set in Regula Antiqua.
The illustrations are pen and ink and watercolor on paper as well as digitally created.
Book design by Carol Goldenberg

Library of Congress Cataloging-in-Publication Data

Brown, Don, 1949–
Odd boy out : young Albert Einstein / by Don Brown.
p. cm.
Summary: An introduction to the work and early life of the twentieth-century physicist
whose theory of relativity revolutionized scientific thinking.
ISBN 0-618-49298-4
PA ISBN 0-547-01435-X
1. Einstein, Albert, 1879-1955–Pictorial works–Juvenile literature.
2. Physicists–Biography–Pictorial works–Juvenile literature.
[1. Einstein, Albert, 1879-1955–Childhood and youth. 2. Physicists.
3. Scientists.] I. Title.
QC16.E5B76 2004
530' .092–dc22
2003017701

Manufactured in China
LEO 10 9 8 7 6
4500419621

For Perf

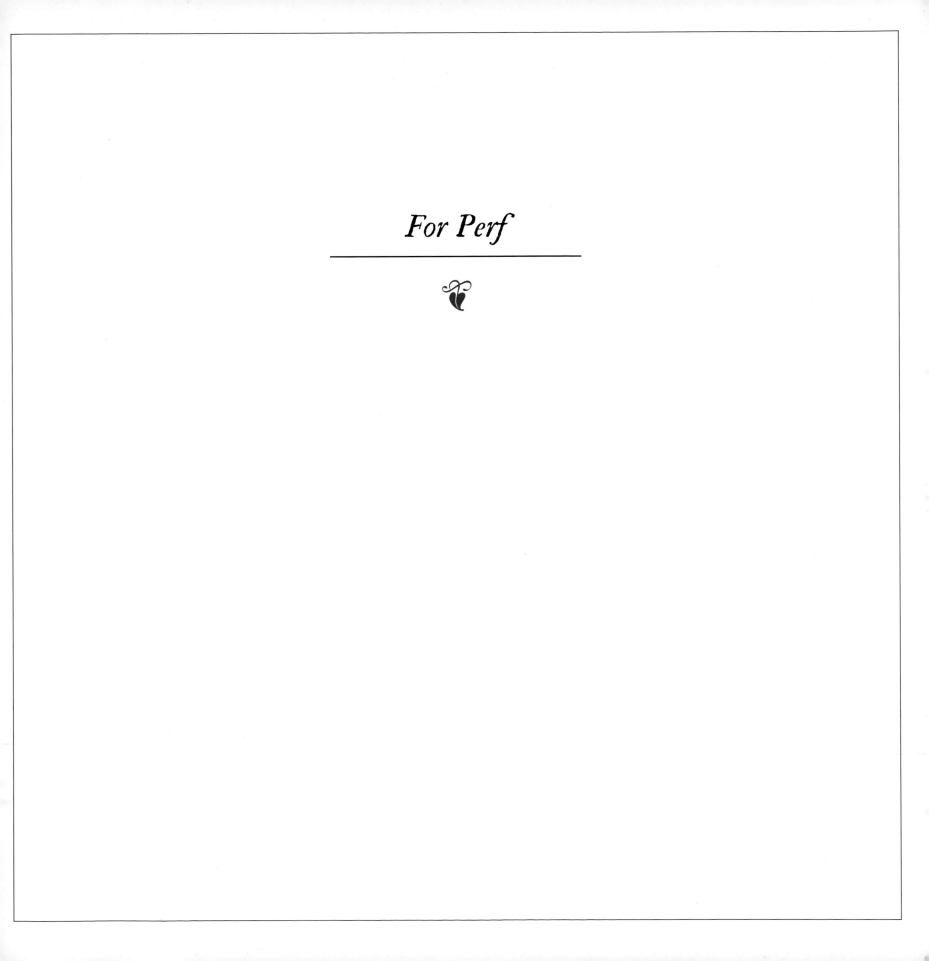

On a sunny, cold Friday in the old city of Ulm, Germany, a baby named Albert Einstein is born. It is March 14, 1879.

The joy his family has for the new birth is brief.

His grandmother cries, "Much too fat. Much too fat."

And his mother fears his head is too big.

Be patient and all will be well, the doctor insists. And he is right, although the back of Albert's head will always appear somehow swollen.

TOO FAT!

Albert grows, and soon it is time for him to coo and babble and make cute words. But he says . . . nothing. His family frets and waits and frets and waits. Is Albert well?

Finally, he talks, and when he does he can be clever and sharp. When he is nearly three, his parents promise Albert a surprise, and he expects a toy. When instead they present him with a baby sister, he says, "Where are the wheels?"

Albert is sometimes cruel to his sister, Maja. He nearly hits her with a hard ball and strikes her head with a hoe. Later Maja would say that one needed a "sound skull" to be Albert's sister.

Poor Maja is not the only object of Albert's anger. Many times when he is displeased, his face pales, his nose goes white, and a nasty tantrum follows. His temper so terrifies a tutor hired to help young Albert prepare for school that she runs away, never to be seen again.

But Albert isn't all anger and brooding. To things he enjoys, he brings a single-minded attention.

Houses of cards captivate him, and he builds one fourteen stories high.

A simple compass, a gift from his father, astonishes Albert. He turns it, tilts it, tips it, and yet the gadget's needle always points north! What "hidden thing" makes it work? he wonders.

The Einsteins move to the large city of Munich. There, Albert's parents encourage his independence and take the unusual step of allowing four-year-old Albert to wander the streets unattended.

He starts school. Among his classmates, he is an odd boy.
The others love to play ball. Albert does not like sports.

Soldiers on parade excite the boys. They disturb Albert.

And Albert is Jewish, the only one of all the students. Some of his classmates taunt and insult him for it.

Young Albert does well in the school subjects that he likes and ignores the others. He likes math. Not so, Latin and Greek.

When questioned in class, Albert lingers over his responses, frustrating his teachers, who prefer quick, snappy answers. And afterward the teachers see his lips move as he quietly repeats the answer to himself.

Is Albert dull-witted? the teachers wonder.

Nevertheless, he earns good grades.

At home, he practices the violin, especially the music of Mozart. No tutor is necessary to keep Albert to this task.

"I believe that love [of a subject] is a better teacher than a sense of duty — at least for me," he later said.

When Albert is twelve, his parents invite a medical student named Max Talmud to their home. He and Albert become friends, a rare thing for Albert, who later described himself as having the "sense of being a stranger with a need for solitude."

Max gives young Albert a geometry book. The exact world of shapes, lines, points, and angles is a wonderwork to him.

"After a short time, a few months, he had worked through the whole book," Max later said. "He thereupon devoted himself to higher mathematics. . . . Soon the flight of his mathematical genius was so high that I could no longer follow."

Unlike the charms of math, other schoolwork bores Albert. The "mindless and mechanical method of teaching caused me great difficulties," he said. "I would rather let all kinds of punishment descend upon me than learn to rattle something off by heart."

His disinterest in schoolwork and distant manner irk some of his teachers.

One tells Albert he would "never get anywhere in life."

Albert ignores the teacher's prediction and occupies himself with music and math. He mulls puzzlements of his own invention. What would it be like to ride a light beam? he wonders. Would the world appear the same if you raced at light's phenomenal speed?

When Albert is about fifteen, his father's business takes the family to Milan, Italy. But before Albert can leave Germany, the law says he must serve in the military. So he is left behind to first complete high school and then the army. Albert moves into a boarding house.

His mood turns black. Albert is miserable at school and longs for the comfort of his family. His happiness and health sink. To recover, he is given special permission to quit school and join the others in Italy.

Life is sunny there. Albert has his family, museums to visit, and, of course, his private study of math. For this, Albert can push everything else from his thoughts, much as he did when he built houses of cards. Even at parties, Albert unravels knotty math problems, unaware of the guests, the talk, and the music.

He tries to enroll in Zurich Polytechnic, a college in Switzerland. But, unprepared in the school subjects he has neglected, Albert fails the entrance test. He spends the next year earning his high school diploma and then enters Polytechnic and trains to be a scientist.

Young Albert graduates and tries to find work teaching at a university, but no job appears. In 1902, he takes the position of Expert III Class at the Swiss patent office, a kind of government library for new inventions.

Albert marries and becomes a father.

The duties of family and work do not stop him from puzzling and wondering. About math. About light. Time. The world. The universe.

Sometimes he pushes his baby son's carriage through the streets of Zurich. Like a night sky filled with stars, Albert's mind is bright with glowing ideas. And as stars are joined into images called constellations, Albert's ideas make a picture of space and time and energy and matter that no one has ever seen before.

Albert says that light is made up of tiny bits of energy called photons that behave like a spray of water from a hose. He says that everything is in motion and when something moves very fast, as fast as light, strange things happen, like clocks running slower and objects becoming shorter. Albert says that something as tiny as a grain of sand is the vessel of unimaginable energy.

For scientists, Albert's discoveries mean the photoelectric effect, theories of relativity, and $E = mc^2$.

For the rest of us, his ideas mean automatic door openers, television, space travel, and atomic energy.

For Albert, his work earns him a great award, the Nobel Prize. He becomes famous, but to him fame is like the hubbub of his parents' parties, something to be ignored while he enjoys wonders and puzzlements of his own invention.

For the world, *Einstein* comes to mean not fat baby, or angry child, or odd boy, but great thinker.

Author's Note

ALBERT EINSTEIN DIED nearly a half-century ago, and yet he and his famous equation, E=mc², remain entrenched in the world's popular thought. Despite this familiarity, many misunderstandings and misconceptions have grown up around Albert Einstein.

E=mc², the equation joining matter and energy, is possibly the most famous equation ever conceived, but it did not earn Einstein the Nobel Prize. In 1921 the prize in physics went to *On the Electrodynamics of Moving Bodies*, Einstein's thoughts concerning the nature of light. That work, as well as E=mc² and the Special Theory of Relativity were all completed in 1905, often referred to as Einstein's *annus mirabilis,* or miracle year. And the miracle wasn't underwritten by a research grant or university stipend but was the product of moments stolen away from his duties as patent examiner, father, and husband.

Einstein did not invent the atom bomb. In 1939, he wrote a letter to President Roosevelt suggesting that the Nazis planned to build one, and proposed the need for more American nuclear research. Nearly disregarded, the letter eventually inspired the Manhattan Project and the task of building an American atomic bomb. But Einstein played no role in its construction and was banned from the project as a security risk for his socialist politics and pacifism.

Albert Einstein died in New Jersey in 1955. The doctor who performed the autopsy to determine the cause of death — heart failure — made off with Einstein's brain and kept it in a jar for more than forty years. Its fate is described in Michael Paterniti's enchanting book *Driving Mr. Albert: A Trip Across America with Einstein's Brain.*

Bibliography

Bodanis, David. *E=mc²: A Biography of the World's Most Famous Equation.* New York: Berkeley Books, 2000.

Brian, Denis. *Einstein: A Life.* New York: John Wiley & Sons, 1996.

Einstein, Albert. *Autobiographical Notes.* Chicago: Open Court Publishing Company, 1979.

Folsing, Albrecht. *Albert Einstein.* New York: Viking, 1997.

Highfield, Roger, and Paul Carter. *The Private Lives of Albert Einstein.* New York: St. Martin's Press, 1993.

Paterniti, Michael. *Driving Mr. Albert: A Trip Across America with Einstein's Brain.* New York: Dial Press, 2000.

Severance, John. *Einstein: Visionary Scientist.* New York: Clarion Books, 1999.